LOGAN'S SECRET

&

Second Edition

SUZANNE BURKE

Burke, Suzanne

    Logan's Secret: A Retired Racing Greyhound's Amazing Secret to Survival/by Suzanne Burke

ISBN-13: 978-1478325383

2nd Edition, August 2012

GREYHOUND STORIES
A Voice for Retired Racing Greyhounds
Dallas, Texas
Email: info@greyhoundstories.com
www.greyhoundstories.com

For information regarding special discounts for bulk purchases, please contact us online at info@greyhoundstories.com

Printed in the United States of America

Logan's Secret Reviews

"I am 7 years old and I LOVED this book!!! I couldn't stop reading it until I was finished! It was AWESOME. I learned a lot about dog racing and animal rescue. It is hard to find shorter chapter books that have pictures like this one." – A Kid's Review – age 7

"Logan's Secret was adventurous. It was so good that I read it with my little sisters again and again. Logan was a hero for himself and for us, too. I can't wait to read about the rest of the greyhound adventures!!!" – A Kid's Review – age 8

"Logan's Secret teaches about decision making, positive thinking, and overcoming challenges-good life lessons for any age. The projects at the end are a unique bonus for children!" – Hemingway

"Logan teaches us that we make our own decisions on whether to be happy or sad and that we can either choose to accept what life dishes out to us, or make the decision to change it. Ms. Burke (and Logan) do an excellent job in presenting us a story that is easy for anyone (young or old) to understand and enjoy." – N. Caponi

"In just a few pages and with elegance, the tough life of a racing greyhound is told, as well as a profound message of hope and perseverance for all of us who face troubled times. I also enjoyed the beautiful photos and illustrations." – J. Accardo

DEDICATION

This book is dedicated to all animal adoption and rescue groups worldwide who work to support animals in need and who help find caring and loving homes for them. I especially want to thank all the Greyhound and Galgo Adoption Groups worldwide who work to home the retired racers at the end of their careers.

To Logan (aka "Rapido USA" and "Sam") — You are my heart and soul. You have taught me so much in your lifetime, but mostly how to love, live in the moment, and assert a positive attitude toward everything. Heartfelt gratitude to you! You are forever in my heart!

To my Family — Mom, Dad, Grandma, Steve, Jeff, Tim, Andy, Sarah, Uncle Bob, Eric, Heidi, Brian, Alecia, Caitlin, Chloe, Liliana, Chrissy, Barbara, Brenda, and Robert, thank you always for your love and belief in my aspirations.

To Doug — Thank you for your love, friendship, and encouragement!

To my friends — Annette, Bill, Brian, Cathy, Cheryl, Claire, Colleen, Don and GeorgeAnn, Joe, John, Jaimie, Kent, Kristin, Lili, Lisa, Mary, Nancy, Sammye, Sara, Sarah, Shawn, Susie, Tim, and Torrey, thank you for your love, inspiration, and support!

From Logan — Thanks to my greyhound family and friends for your love and friendship! Thank you Allie, Amber, Annie, Ari, Big D Dale, Blaze, Blue, Buddy, Bugsy, Bully and Nelson, Cassie, Cheyenne, Ci, Dolce, Duke, Edu, Friday, Hayley, Huston, Jack, Marvin, Patch, Promise, Tony, Tricky, and too many more to mention here.

Blaze

Dale

A special dedication to Blaze (aka "Chasen Blaze") and Big D Dale ("Cry Dale"), who left this earth during the writing of this book! Run free, my sweet boys, you will both be terribly missed!

SUZANNE BURKE

CONTENTS

ACKNOWLEDGMENTS

To The Greyhound Adoption League of Texas — Thank you for your support. Your motto, "No Grey Turned Away," speaks volumes about your love and support for all greyhounds. You always find a way to support the most challenging greyhound cases, and the outcome is always heartening. The volunteers are truly awe-inspiring!

To the staffs at VCA Preston Park Animal Hospital, Cross Timbers Animal Medical Center, VCA Dallas Veterinary Surgical Center, and VCA Animal Diagnostic Clinic — You are the miracle workers! Thank you for your hard work and dedication to the greyhounds and other furry friends!

Thanks to Shawn Fernandez Media Works, Shannon Forrest, and John Hudson Photography for your creative photographs.

❧❦

"He is your friend, your partner, your defender, your dog. You are his life, his love, his leader. He will be yours, faithful and true, to the last beat of his heart. You owe it to him to be worthy of such devotion."
– Unknown

"All our dreams can come true, if we have the courage to pursue them."
– Walt Disney

CHAPTER 1
❧❧

THE GREYHOUND

I could feel the cool, gritty sand beneath my calloused paws as slivers of sunlight danced through the slats of my start box. The excited yelps of other greyhounds echoed all around me. My heart pounded rapidly in my chest; it was almost race time!

My name is Logan. I'm a greyhound, an elite racing greyhound. During my racing career, my name was Rapido USA. I come from a family of racing greyhounds; all my family members had Rapido or Oshkosh as part of their names. Rapido is Spanish for fast. And, boy, are we greyhounds fast! We can sprint up to 45 miles per hour!

Logan (aka "Rapido USA")

When we run, it's almost as if we can fly, with our feet high off the ground. We can run around a quarter-mile track in half a minute. That's 30 seconds!

Although running is fun and I was *really* good at it, my job was to win.

The more races I won, the more money my owner won, and the more treats and petting I received. Every greyhound in line beside me at the starting gate wanted to win just as much as I did, which is why we were all so excited to start the race. We all pushed and strained for the first glimpse of our target: the rabbit.

Sure, we were all friends between races, but during the race that friendship was replaced by frenzied competition.

Our focus shifted to just one thing—chasing the rabbit around the track!

Whoever chased the rabbit the fastest would be the first to cross the finish line.

And the first across the finish line was the winner! The winner would be showered with treats, and the people who bet on the fastest greyhound would be showered with money!

I wanted to be the winner! I *always* wanted to be the winner!

Every racer wanted to be the winner, so the competition was fierce, which is why we all had to wear muzzles during the race.

We got so excited and competitive while chasing the rabbit that we tried to bite and bump each other to become the leader in the race and win! Being a racing greyhound was hard and grueling work. Winning races made my owner happy and made me proud.

But, I sometimes wondered whether there was more to life than racing, or even winning. I'd heard stories about greyhounds "retiring" and moving to "forever homes." I didn't really know what that meant, but it fascinated me just the same.

CLANG, CLANG, CLANG! The bell rang!

No time to wonder about that now. The race was on!

CHAPTER 2

࿇࿇

THE RACE

The race box starting gates flew open. We launched ourselves like rockets, and were off and running to the roar of the crowd! Our lean, muscled bodies stretched and strained as we jockeyed for position. Sand flew, as our paws dug deeply into the track. We were eight wild-eyed competitors, crashing and colliding into each other, sprinting at full speed.

Today's strategy was to run the inside lane. It was the shortest path to winning. It was also the toughest, because all eight of us wanted to run the same inside lane.

I was running in the lead with a breakaway pack of two other dogs, but there were still five others, hot on our tails!

As we bunched ever more tightly together through the first turn, the rabbit just beyond our muzzled reach, the strangest thing happened! For a moment—and only a moment—a question popped into my head: "Why am I doing this?" Then another! "Is this all there is?"

By the time I snapped back to reality—it was only a second or two later—I'd already slipped to the rear of the pack. I was eating their dust!

Returning my focus to the race, I pushed my muscles to the limit, quickly passed the rear pack, and closed in on the two leaders.

Faking a left-move to the inside rail, they tried to block me. I tricked them and exploded to the outside, easily passing them both, sand flying into their faces!

I was now in first place! But, not for long...

"Forever home!" It was happening again! My mind was wandering again!

Except this time it wasn't a question. It was a vision, a vision I could see as clearly as the rabbit on the rail—a forever home with a soft, fluffy bed and humans who loved me all the time, not just when I won a race.

I slowed down. Other dogs passed me. I slipped back into the pack and then to the rear of the pack.

My thoughts came back to me. "I've worked so hard, training and racing for years. I've earned this dream! I deserve a forever home! I want a forever home!"

Then, I just stopped in my tracks. I stopped running and slowly walked, my head held down.

I could hear people calling out from the grandstand.

"What's wrong with that dog?" "Is he hurt?"

"Run, you mangy mutt! I've got 20 bucks bet on you!"

I had let everybody down. Maybe I even let myself down.

My mind was a blur of emotions. I felt uncertain, fearful, and even a little crazy. My owner was going to be so angry! But, more than anything else, I now felt at peace for the first time in my life. I knew I was finished racing. I knew I was going to have a forever home. I just didn't know how.

CHAPTER 3

∂∾⊶

RAPIDO USA RETIRES

As I walked slowly toward my owner, he looked at me and said, "Rapido USA, you've lost your edge! You have to retire. Your heart is just not into racing anymore!"

Reality hit me again, and thoughts came flooding into my mind. "Racing was all I have ever known! This is the only home I have ever really known! What will happen to me? Where will I go?"

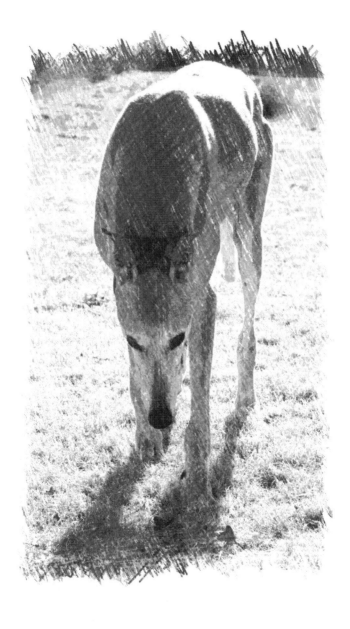

I trembled with fear at my decision to stop in the middle of the race. Was it the right one? I just didn't know.

I acted on impulse, because I believed the only way I could change my life *was* to make a dramatic change during that race. I thought that stopping would help get me retired to that "forever home" with the soft, fluffy bed, loving family, yummy food, and toys! But what if I was wrong? What if I was shipped to another racetrack far away where I didn't know anyone?

That evening, I was moved to a different kennel away from the elite racing greyhounds. Although the new space was larger, it was old and tattered and smelled musty and moldy.

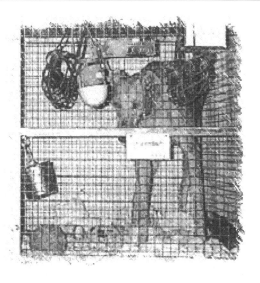

As I lay in the unfamiliar kennel on a bed of shredded newspaper, I had no idea what would happen next. I was truly scared!

Because my owner thought I had given up, he retired me. Soon, he shipped me off to a greyhound adoption group in a far-away city, a place where "retirement" for ex-greyhound racers begins.

I was about to embark on a new life journey, and it started with me inside a special greyhound trailer, traveling from Florida to Texas.

When I arrived at the greyhound adoption group, they treated me like a king! They were gentle and loving. They bathed me and made me feel brand new! They gave me a new name too: *Sam*.

I had a bed. It wasn't the fluffy one I had dreamed about, but it was better than the shredded newspaper in my old crate at the racetrack.

The new kennel had a large dog run, too, where I could go outside or come inside anytime I wanted.

Perhaps I did make the right choice to stop that day during the race.

CHAPTER 4
༄༅

THE ADOPTION

The following week, after I had a health checkup, the greyhound adoption group placed me in a foster home with a very kind family, complete with two lively children. Greyhounds stay with foster families until someone picks them for a forever home.

The children and I would play all day, and we had so much fun together.

I had a big, soft, fluffy bed on which to rest, and there were toys, too! The food was delicious, with plenty of extra treats. Was this my dream home? I sure thought so.

My foster family took me to weekly events, called Meet and Greets, where people come to meet you to see whether they want to adopt you. This was where we greyhounds received lots of attention from the visitors. The visitors would talk to us, pet us, and give us scrumptious treats. I especially loved these events, because everyone was so lively and happy.

After only one month of Meet and Greets, I was finally chosen and adopted by a sweet, quiet woman who lived in the countryside.

CHAPTER 5
ക൪ക

THE ESCAPE

My new mom and I got along fine
for a while, but there was a sadness
about her, and it seemed I couldn't make
her happy. I wanted her to play with me
and my new squeaky toys. I wanted her
to watch me run around the yard and
throw me balls to chase. Sometimes, I
would do twirls to get her attention.
Other times, I would bark to get her
attention, thinking, "Come on, Mom,
let's go play!"

I tried and tried, but I suppose she didn't have much time for me.

I so wanted to be in a home where people expressed love, were happy, and wanted to spend time with me, like my foster home with the two children.

I saw an open backyard gate one day and I wandered outside. I turned around to look for my mom, but she didn't come after me, so I just kept walking.

I was plodding along, trying to figure out where I would go next. I wandered down a quiet country road thinking about my dream home, when an older woman in a blue car stopped and asked whether I was lost.

I wanted to tell her, "No, I'm not lost—I'm just searching for my forever home!"

She invited me into her car, and amazingly, she brought me back to the greyhound adoption group! I couldn't believe my luck! Maybe they would find me a happier home, like my foster home.

Well, guess what? I got to return to my old foster home that evening, to the two little children who were so much fun! We loved playing together. They would toss me balls, and I would happily bring them back with slobber all over them. They would exclaim, "Oh Sam, you slobbered on the ball again!" I don't think it really bothered them, because they kept throwing it. We would play and laugh until we were exhausted! I even let them take turns riding on me like a pony, although my foster mom was never happy about that. You know what? My dream of returning to my foster home did come true, didn't it?

I was very happy with my foster family, and I never planned to leave. But, one day, I noticed the backyard gate was cracked open just a little.

I looked at all the open space beyond and wondered, "Hmm, what's it like outside the gate? Maybe I'll just venture out for a little bit to see what's going on." So I did just that!

I strolled around the neighborhood, gazing at all the activity. There were so many beautiful flowers and trees beginning to bloom with the hint of spring. There was also an abundance of squirrels with big, fat, fluffy tails. I even chased a few of the squirrels, but they were too crafty and were able to sprint across the yards and up trees, where I couldn't catch them.

I felt so free though with no leash. I was just a vagabond wandering to who knows where on a balmy sunny day! How did I know I would not be able to find my way back home?

I wandered around for days in the big city, trying to find my home, but I couldn't remember where it was. My stomach rumbled with hunger! I thought, "If I could only find some food, I could keep traveling to find my home."

Then, one morning, I heard children playing. I slowly followed the playful voices, and found a schoolyard. I thought for a moment, "Hey, wasn't my home near here?"

I wondered whether my foster family was here. I walked up to a few children looking for my foster family, but I didn't see them. All the kids wanted to pet me, so I stopped to receive a few pats on the head. I looked up to one child, begging him with my eyes and chattering teeth to help me find my home, but the child couldn't understand what I wanted. He petted me for a moment, then ran off to play with his friends.

"How will I ever find my foster home?" I cried to myself. Scared, starving, thirsty and most of all, tired from all the walking, I begged for help from above! If I could find my home, I could get some food and return to my warm, fluffy bed!

Someone must have heard my plea, because it was then that a man with a cowboy hat walked up to me, bent down, and asked in a gruff voice, "Boy, are you lost?"

"Well, yes I am," I wanted to say. I tried to speak with my eyes to tell him,

"Please, take me back to my home—I just want to go home!"

Sadly, the cowboy couldn't understand my thoughts either. He asked me to jump in his pickup truck, which I gladly did, because I was starving and just wanted to go home. As we drove in his pickup truck, I wondered where we were going.

He said, "Boy, I just want to get you out of harm's way. The city is no place for a dog like you."

I wanted to cry out, "Hey, my name is Sam. I know I live just around the corner. Can't you take me to my home?"

CHAPTER 6
ॐॐ

THE RANCH

We drove for what seemed like an eternity through the big city, and then rumbled down country roads, thick with pine trees, taking us deep into the country. Was I going back to the sad woman from my first home? I was so confused and extremely worried. This wasn't anything I had pictured in my daydreams! Where were the soft, fluffy bed and the loving family from my dream?

When we arrived at the man's ranch, I saw the large house and thought, "Hey this isn't so bad! I bet there's a big, fluffy bed inside there.

And, look at all that land where I would be able to run! I bet there are toys and delicious food in there, too!"

This place looked like pure paradise to me. My fear turned to excitement over the prospect that I may just have found my "forever home." Oh boy, this was going to be awesome!

When the cowboy took me to the backyard and stuck me in an old rusty cage, I knew I was in trouble. Not only was my home a rusty cage, instead of a fluffy, soft bed, everything else was all wrong, too! Instead of the rigid schedule we kept at the race kennel— breakfast early in the morning, exercise and training during the day, regular breaks to go to the bathroom, and dinner in the evening—I never knew when the rancher was going to feed me or let me out of my cage.

At the ranch, my stomach rumbled constantly, because I was starving most of the time, never getting enough food. The water was dirty and tasted old, but I drank it to stay alive. The rancher didn't feed me very much at all, and he told me I had to be starving so I would be good and hungry to hunt.

"Hunt? What was I going to hunt?" I thought to myself. I wasn't good at hunting; I only knew how to race!"

One day at dawn, the gruff rancher opened my cramped cage and announced, "Boy, we're going huntin' for rabbit." I rolled my eyes, thinking this was going to be a waste of energy. He made me walk the ranch and when he saw a rabbit, he'd yell at me, "Go get em, boy!"

Okay, I admit it was fun chasing after the rabbits, but I would always let them escape, secretly snickering every time they got away.

The rancher would get so mad and yell at me, "Catch the darned rabbit, you goofy dog!" I didn't like this man, and catching rabbits would be a miserable waste of my life! I didn't want to kill rabbits, and I sure didn't want to live on this ranch. I should have run away when I had a chance during those hunting trips, but I was afraid I would starve, like when I was lost in the city. The country was so vast, and there were no other houses around, so I had no clue how to survive on my own out there. I felt so defeated! How was I going to change this nightmarish life I was living? I was a caged prisoner!

During my time on the ranch, I weathered many horrific thunderstorms. They were terrifying! The powerful crashing of thunder, the blinding lightning bolts, and heavy rain pounding on top of me made me shiver and cower in the cold, wet cage.

"What did I do to deserve this?" I wondered. I had no greyhound buddies to talk to, and there were no children to play with.

I had barely enough food and clean water to survive. I was left outside in a hard, cold, wet cage, and it was freezing at night.

I was scared and lonely and in deep despair, wondering how I was going to get out of this mess! I wondered, "Did I make the right decision by stopping in the middle of the race that day?"

After weeks of being afraid and feeling sorry for myself, I knew I had to change my way of thinking.

A new idea occurred to me: "If I think positively, instead of worrying about my current situation and whether I made the right decision at the race track that fateful day, my situation could quite possibly change!"

Instead of thinking about *how* I was going to get to my forever home, I needed to be clear about *what* I wanted.

I should imagine my dream home in my mind and then visualize it, like when we visualized winning our races.

Imagining my new life with the soft, fluffy bed, delicious tidbits, and a loving family would take me further toward my goal of the perfect forever home, right? I had to have faith that I would find it someday!

I began to imagine the dream in my mind. I dreamed of the big, soft, fluffy bed most of all, because my bones ached immensely from lying on the cold, hard cage floor. I needed to believe this dream would come true, because that's the only way I saw my situation changing. It was my way of surviving day to day on this miserable ranch.

CHAPTER 7

❧❧

THE VISITOR

One chilly morning, after countless weeks of lying in the cage, a woman with a bright red coat came to visit the rancher. I heard her footsteps as she approached my cage. The rancher let me out so I could stretch my muscles and walk around a bit. Boy, did it feel good to stretch my tired, cramped legs each time I was allowed out!

I overheard the woman ask the rancher what he was going to do with me. As I listened intently to their conversation, I realized she was trying to get me out of there! After their brief exchange, she left as suddenly as she came, but I clearly remember one thing from her visit. She came up to me and said, "Boy, I am going to find a home for you, so don't give up."

That one little piece of hope was something I could hold onto, a reason to keep my dream alive. I decided I must continue to visualize my forever home — the one with the soft, fluffy bed, toys, yummy food, and a family to love me. I dreamed about it for days.

CHAPTER 8
꙳

THE VISION

Several weeks later, on a very cold night, I awoke from a restless sleep outside in the cage. I was freezing and my body ached from the cold, hard cage floor. Half asleep, my eyes peeked open; I saw a faint, blurred image of a person. It wasn't the woman in the bright red coat who promised to find me a home, but someone different.

This person was a woman with long, dark hair, sparkling blue eyes, and a welcoming smile. She seemed to speak to me from a far-off distance, like an echo, telling me she was looking for me. Who was she?

The vision was mesmerizing, and I couldn't erase it from my mind. Somehow, it brought me peace.

With each passing slumber, the vision and dreams of this person became more real. Each time, she whispered to me that she was looking for me, and my forever home would be there when I was ready. I began to think of her as my guardian angel.

The weeks continued to drag on, and I kept having dreams of this angel rescuing me. Although the dreams were mysterious, they brought me comfort and gave me a warm, secure feeling.

A rabbit visited me one night after my vision of the woman with the sparkling blue eyes. He approached my cage with caution, sniffing around. I lay quietly watching as he foraged for food. The rabbit looked so innocent. He was just a little thing and was without his mother.

I wondered why he was all alone. He looked hungry, like when I was lost for days in the city. That seemed like such a long time ago. I instantly felt guilt about chasing all those rabbits the rancher made me hunt.

What if one of the rabbits I chased was his mother? What if I scared her half to death and she ran off leaving this poor lost rabbit alone to fend for himself?

Something occurred to me that night. As young greyhounds, we were taught to hunt rabbits; they were our enemies. However, we never knew the rabbits personally. We were never given a chance to meet one face-to-face and form a friendship.

Each generation of greyhounds was taught to hate rabbits and chase and kill them. Why should I hate this rabbit? He didn't do anything to me. He seemed so innocent and happy.

The rabbit began to visit me nightly, as if he could sense my extreme loneliness. Although we couldn't really communicate, we both silently understood we were developing a bond. I even named him! I called my new friend Jack!

The rabbit was there to keep me company, as I lay a prisoner in the cage night after night. I welcomed his visits each night as he sniffed around my cage, and I thought, "Maybe I was there to help him learn that not all greyhounds are bad."

One evening at dusk, the rabbit came to visit, but he was early this time. He usually didn't appear until much later, when it was pitch dark. I thought this odd but was happy to see him anyway. I could see him much more clearly in the dusk's amber light. He was tiny, with fluffy, brown-tipped fur and a little white cottontail. He approached my cage with more ease that evening, tail wiggling.

Sensing he was not in any danger, he sniffed more closely to the gate of my cage, and this time he let me sniff him. He smelled of fresh green clover, and he seemed at peace with my friendly offering of a sniff back at him. He sat beside the cage with me as we both shared the rose-colored hue of the setting sun.

As we watched the sun set over the green rolling hills of the ranch, I noticed clouds forming a fluffy white shape bathed in golden light.

The cloud had an unusual shape, but I couldn't make out what it was exactly. It seemed to have some meaning, because I felt a warm energy wash over my body.

The rabbit seemed to be gazing at the same image, and we both stared at it, unblinking. He turned back and looked at me straight into my eyes, twinkled his whiskered nose, then scampered away as the sun melted into the landscape. I wondered what all this meant—the setting sun, the image in the cloud, and the warm rush of energy bathing my body. It was as if something wonderful were about to happen. I fell asleep that night feeling very peaceful and happy for the first time in many weeks!

CHAPTER 9

❧⚛

THE RESCUE

The next day, the sun rose with all its splendor, its light spreading slowly across the dewy landscape. I awoke from one of my recurring dreams and, for some reason, I felt happy and peaceful. I knew something big was going to happen that day. The air had a scent of freshly mowed grass, and it smelled so clean. I felt a tingling energy all around me. I wanted to get out of the cage to stretch my aching muscles and shake my fur to remove the dust.

Just then, I heard a car drive up to the front of the house. The car door opened and then shut. I could hear the crunching footsteps and the muffled voices of the rancher and a woman. Was it the woman in the bright red coat that promised to help me, or was it my guardian angel with the long dark hair and sparkling blue eyes from my many dreams?

Walking toward my cage the rancher bent down, looked at me, and said gruffly, "Boy, we found whom you belong to. You're going home."

"Wow," I thought, amazingly. "This is a miracle! I am finally going to my forever home!"

My tail slapped the cage with incredible delight; I was so excited with the promise of finally being free!

The rancher released me from the cage, and I shook all the dust from my fur and stretched long and lean.

It felt so good, and I felt more alive than I had in many weeks!

The rancher said his goodbyes and escorted me to the woman. My tail wagged with such excitement at the idea that I was rescued!

As I looked up at the aging woman, I realized this wasn't the familiar woman with the long, dark hair and sparkling blue eyes from my dreams.

And, it wasn't the woman with the bright red coat who promised to find a home. This was a completely different woman!

Who was she? Where was I going? How was I going to find the woman from my dreams and my forever home? I made the decision to stop worrying about something that had not even happened. Once again, I decided to focus on *what* I did want!

My instinct told me to trust this woman and not to worry, so I climbed into the car.

We rumbled down the country roads to the highway and back through the big city.

My dream came back to me, so I held
onto it in my mind, thinking of a
positive outcome as I lay with my head
on my paws.

CHAPTER 10
ᘒᘓ

THE MEETING

We finally arrived at a building, which looked familiar to me. Hey, I had been here before! It was the office of a veterinarian, a doctor for pets. This was the place I had gone to get my checkup when I first arrived from the racetrack. Still a little scared, I climbed out of the car, my legs wobbly.

As we entered the vet's office, I saw the same people from the greyhound adoption group who took me in when I first arrived! They were talking among themselves and seemed very glad to see me!

I looked at each person's face, but I didn't see the woman with the long, dark hair and sparkling blue eyes from my dreams. I felt certain she would be here! Why wasn't she here?

Panicked, I wondered where she was. Would my guardian angel ever come for me? Was she even real? Why did I dream about her every night?

I sank down and rested my head on my paws, feeling so discouraged. Where would I go now?

As I lay there on the cold tile floor wondering about all that happened during the past few weeks, I wondered why I ended up here. What would be the next chapter in my journey as a retired racer?

I slowly turned my head to gaze at the volunteers. Scanning each of their faces, I wondered whether any of them would take me home. Just as my mind again drifted off to the woman in my dream, I heard a soft voice speak as someone came through the front door. Was I dreaming again? The voice exclaimed, "Sam, there you are!"

As I turned to look, it was the woman I had dreamed about!

She had long, dark hair and sparkling blue eyes! I sprang to my feet. She had come for me! I shook my fur and began chattering my teeth with excitement as she gracefully walked toward me.

She gently knelt down, put her arms around me and said with a big smile, "Sam, this is a miracle! We've been searching for you for weeks, and here you are!" She hugged me tightly and kissed me, tears rolling down her cheeks!

Was this my new mom? Was she taking me to my forever home? I was so overjoyed to see her; I slapped big, sloppy dog-kisses all over her face!

She looked exactly as I pictured her! I desperately hoped she would understand that my kisses meant I wanted to go home with her.

After getting checked out by the vet and receiving a clean bill of health, my guardian angel with the long, dark hair and sparkling blue eyes whisked me away to her car and drove me to her home, just as I had imagined in my mind. It was amazing how visualizing my dreams had really worked!

CHAPTER 11
ಶಿ‑ೀ

THE FOREVER HOME

We arrived a short time later at my new foster home. It was a warm, loving home with soft, fluffy beds everywhere! There were fat, furry toys to play with and the most scrumptious, lip-smacking food you could ever imagine!

There was a huge backyard filled with cool green grass, plenty of oak trees, squirrels, and beautiful fragrant flowers. It was the most awesome place to run and stretch my legs. Best of all, there

were other greyhounds there! I had
really missed my greyhound friends from
the racetrack, and having new friends
was the best thing I could have
imagined!

This was paradise! It was peaceful
and happy. It was the perfect place to
rest my weary bones. I thought, happily,

"I found my forever home. I want to live my retired life right here!"

In the evening, I met my new foster mom's husband. As I was resting comfortably inside my dream home on a big, soft, fluffy bed, I heard her ask him, "Can we adopt Sam? Please? We spent more than six weeks looking for him, and it's a miracle he was found. I know he belongs here with us as part of our family!"

I peered slowly out of the corner of my eye, my teeth chattering with excitement waiting to hear his response. I was screaming to myself, "Say yes, say yes! I know this is my forever home!" Then, he turned to her smiling and said, "Of course we can!"

"Yippee!" I yelled to myself, tail wagging.

I sprang from my bed and did my best happy greyhound dance, twirling around in circles, to show them my extreme excitement and gratitude. They both laughed and hugged me tightly! That night, I was adopted into my "forever home," my dream home!

I kept my focus on what I wanted and visualized it in my mind, like how we were taught to visualize winning our races. Although I was a little impatient about the timing of finding my dream home, I now see that all of the people and events were coming together one by one to help me find the perfect home. I just needed to have faith that it would come true.

By the way, I now have a new friend. I named him Jack, after the rabbit that was such a comfort to me at the ranch. Jack and I are inseparable. My new name is Logan, and I am a happily retired racing greyhound!

CHAPTER 12

ॐॐ

THE SECRET MESSAGE

Here's the secret I learned during my journey: *Your thoughts make a big difference in how life turns out.* Both good and bad thoughts are powerful, and the kinds of thoughts and words you send out, you receive back. If you worry about something that hasn't happened, you may attract it. On the other hand, if you send out good thoughts and words, and you treat people and animals kindly, you will attract good things.

After a while, I chose to think good thoughts and visualized what I wanted, instead of what I didn't want. That's what made the difference!

Although it seemed to take a long time to find my forever home, I never gave up hope that I would find it. I kept my dream home alive by visualizing it and believing it would come to me, even through all the challenges I faced on my long journey.

I'm an old greyhound now, and I do not regret what I did that day during my last race, because it opened the door to a better life for me!

Dream your dreams, imagine your dreams often, and make them come alive in your mind! Try sending out only positive thoughts. Your dreams can come true! They truly can! Mine did!

 Logan

CHAPTER 13

❧❧

EPILOGUE

Logan's story is based upon real events that occurred between August 2004 and May 2005. Logan (aka "Rapido USA") was born July 24, 2000 in Texas. He comes from a long line of champions, reaching back to 1780, including several winners of the famed Waterloo Cup during the nineteenth century in England.

Logan was trained to race in Texas, and then moved to Florida to begin his racing career.

After running 152 races in his two-year career from 2002 to 2004, Logan stopped in mid-race during his last race on August 15, 2004, at the Jacksonville Circuit racetrack in Jacksonville, Florida. Ironically, he won his previous race on August 11, coming in first at 31.44 seconds. He was retired at age four and returned from Florida to the kennel in Texas where he was born.

He remained there for a few months and was retired to the Greyhound Adoption League of Texas (GALT) in Dallas, Texas, in late December 2004. There, he was given the new name of Sam. For two months, Sam lived in a foster home in Dallas, awaiting his forever home.

In February 2005, Sam was adopted to a home in North Texas. In early March, he escaped from his adopted home and was found by a Good Samaritan, as he wandered a country road in that area. Sam was returned to the Greyhound Adoption League of Texas and then to his previous foster home in Dallas. One week later, he escaped through an open backyard gate—every dog owner's nightmare.

The foster family and Greyhound Adoption League of Texas volunteers worked tirelessly, posting flyers in the Dallas area where he escaped, and they followed up on every lead.

Sam soon became well known in the lake community as the "Missing Greyhound." Everyone in the community would ask the volunteers about him. Special greyhound walks around the lake were held almost every weekend while Sam was missing to spread awareness about the missing greyhound. The GALT volunteers held searches for six weeks to find Sam.

The GALT volunteers and author Suzanne Burke did not give up hope or lose faith that Sam would be found during the period he was gone, even after leads began to taper off.

A humane trap was set up in the lake community area where he had been reported as seen, and volunteers worked mornings and evenings replenishing food and checking the trap daily hoping to capture Sam.

When the volunteers had just about given up all hope and leads had completely dried up, Suzanne and another woman volunteer were sitting by the lake on a Thursday evening in May at dusk after setting up the trap for the evening.

As the two women sat quietly gazing at the sunset over the lake, both individuals noticed a slowly forming cloud in front of the setting sun.

They were amazed at what they saw and each checked with the other to ensure they were seeing the same thing. The cloud formation was that of a greyhound's head—the image was very distinct, with a long, needle-nosed snout and relaxed ears.

The two women questioned its meaning. They both thought quite possibly that Sam may have crossed over to the other side or would be found soon. Both women walked away that evening numb, with many questions following their visual experience. What could the cloud image possibly mean?

The next day, Friday at noon, a GALT volunteer received a call that Sam had been found on a ranch in Lancaster, Texas, approximately 30 miles south of where he had originally escaped.

The "woman in the bright red coat" had contacted a greyhound rescuer in Fort Worth, who ironically knew one of the GALT volunteers and knew about the missing greyhound. The

Fort Worth greyhound rescuer immediately arranged to have Sam delivered to her care. His positive identity was confirmed by the matching tattoo registration numbers in Sam's left ear.

The events recounted in this story are based on interviews conducted with the ranch owner and the woman in the bright red coat, who visited the ranch and promised to find Sam a home.

The ranch owner had picked up Sam just four days after he escaped from his foster home in Dallas.

Although leads came in frequently about sightings of Sam over a six-week period, we now know this was impossible after the first four days he was missing, since at this point, he was on the ranch in Lancaster. Perhaps a higher source was speaking to the volunteers to keep them hopeful through the many phone calls received about false sightings.

We shall never know, but one thing is certain. This story is a true testament to never give up hope, and to remain persistent and optimistic, believing there is a higher power at work to help us through life's challenges.

During the time that Sam lived on the ranch, Suzanne frequently spoke to him, asking Sam to show himself. He did so in multiple vivid dreams Suzanne had during the period he was missing. Suzanne and the other volunteers never gave up their faith that Sam would be found and, true enough, he was found the day after the two women saw his image in a cloud.

Sam did show himself while missing, only in ways that were different from expected.

As a start to his new life, Suzanne decided to give Sam a new name. After trying out many names, Logan was the only name that elicited a tail wag.

Although much of Logan's story is verifiable, some events were not. We chose to use Logan's point of view to create some of what we don't know.

Today, Logan lives in Dallas with his greyhound brothers and sisters. Suzanne, Logan's mom, continues to be an active volunteer for the Greyhound Adoption League of Texas, a non-profit greyhound adoption group known nationally for its motto: *No Grey Turned Away.*

Look for more true retired racing greyhound stories—as told by the greyhounds themselves—about the challenges they experience in their racing careers, finding their forever homes, and their exciting adventures during retirement!

THE END

ABOUT GREYHOUNDS
ᐛᐛ

Did you know that the greyhound is the fastest breed of dog? Greyhounds can sprint up to 45 miles per hour in three to four strides. They are sighthounds, which mean they use their eyes more than any other part of their body to hunt. A greyhound's heart is as large as a human's heart. They have large muscles in their hindquarters that help to propel them faster while running, and all four legs come off the ground during a run. Their long thin tail is used like a rudder to help steer and to balance them while running.

Because they have only about sixteen percent body fat, they do not have normal dog odor as other breeds that have twice the body fat.

The greyhound is the first dog mentioned in literature. In Greek literature, a book called *The Odyssey* from around 800 BC told a story of a man named Odysseus who left home for 20 years. When he arrived home, the only one who recognized him was his greyhound, "Argus," who was only a puppy when he left home.

The greyhound is the only breed of dog mentioned in the Bible (King James version, Proverbs 30:29-31):

"There be three things which do well, yea, Which are comely in going; A lion, which is strongest among beasts and Turneth not away from any; A greyhound; And a he goat also; and a king, against whom there is no rising up."

Greyhound History

Greyhounds reach back into history more than 8,000 years. Drawings dating back to 6000 B.C. were first found of greyhound like dogs at Çatal Hüyük in Turkey. Greyhounds were popular in Ancient Egypt, and their owners worshiped them almost as much as their children. Egyptians regarded a greyhound so highly that they were considered second in importance to the first-born male child. When a family greyhound died, the family would go into mourning as they would the loss of any family member. Favorite family greyhounds were often buried and mummified in the tombs of their owners upon their deaths. The owners' tombs were frequently decorated with drawings of these favorite greyhounds.

The ancient Greeks loved greyhounds, as well, and probably bought greyhounds from the Egyptians. The Romans acquired them from the Greeks. The Romans then imported them to Europe. From there, greyhounds became favorite pets of many Europeans.

Because greyhounds are excellent hunters, due to their speed and agility, they were used for fox and hare hunting as a sport throughout Europe.

Despite their popularity in Europe, greyhounds were in danger of extinction during the Middle Ages (500s to 1500) as a result of the famine and plague.

Dogs, in general, were looked down upon during the Middle Ages, but the greyhound was considered highly valued, most likely due its agility and ability to hunt.

This was the time period of castles and knights. In tombs, greyhounds were depicted as symbols of knighthood along with the lion to symbolize strength.

Plzen Coat of Arms depicting a greyhound

The greyhound was so valued that monks saved them from starvation and bred them to sell to royal and noble gentlemen, which certainly helped to preserve the breed.

In 1016, King Canute of England enacted a law prohibiting any "common" person from owning a greyhound.

Commoners found owning greyhounds were severely punished. Only aristocracy was allowed to own a greyhound during this era. This held true until around 1700.

During this same period, King Howel of Wales enacted a law that promised the execution for any person killing a greyhound.

Throughout the Renaissance period (1300s to 1600), a period of art renewal, greyhounds often were included in paintings, many times as the focus of the piece.

Several artists, such as Veronese, Pisanello, and Uccello, celebrated greyhounds in their artwork.

Pisanello's "The Vision of Saint Eustace"

Greyhounds remained popular among royalty during the Victorian Era (1837 to 1901). Britain's Prince Albert and Queen Victoria owned many greyhounds. A female greyhound, named Eos was a favorite of Prince Albert, who had owned her since he was fourteen. Prince Albert took Eos with him when he went to live at Buckingham Palace at age 21 after he married Queen Victoria. Eos was seven years old then and lived to age eleven. Many artists captured Eos's beauty, including painter John Lindsey Lucas.

But, the Victorian Era also changed society. Common people were allowed to move upward in status, and any person was permitted to own greyhounds and participate in the sport of coursing.

Portrait of Prince Albert and the Royal
Princess Victoria with their greyhound, Eos,
by John Lindsey Lucas – 1843

Coursing involved releasing two greyhounds to chase a hare (rabbit) in a field to see which dog was the fastest and could best maneuver the corners while chasing.

Many of these coursing events, such as the Waterloo Cup, were highly regarded sporting events.

This three-day event was run each year in Lancashire, England, from 1836 to 2005 (169 years).

Just after the 2005 cup, Parliament passed the Hunting Act 2004, making hare coursing events illegal in England and Wales. The Waterloo cup ended as a result.

Greyhound Racing

In addition to coursing, British sportsmen of the Victorian Era attempted a different kind of greyhound racing.

In 1876, a group of dog owners set up a straight track with an artificial lure for six greyhounds to chase in a straight line. But, their efforts fell flat, and the sport never took off.

In fact, aside from coursing events, greyhounds were not raced successfully until 1926, when Owen Patrick Smith of Emeryville, California, invented an artificial rabbit lure that moved around a circular racetrack.

Smith went on to open more racetracks across the United States, and greyhound racing gained in popularity as a spectator sport from the 1930s to the 1990s in all parts of the world, including America, Europe, and Australia.

By the 1990s, however, greyhound racing began its decline in popularity in the United States, as other types of betting became more popular.

Greyhounds in America

Greyhounds first migrated to the Americas in what is now New Mexico with Spanish settlers as early as the 1500s and were used to guard and hunt.

Some famous explorers who had greyhounds were Christopher Columbus, Ponce De Leon, Vasco Nuñez de Balboa, and Hernán Cortés.

We don't catch up with greyhounds again in American historical writings until the Colonial period. Baron Von Stueben, who was the famous Prussian Major General of the Continental Army during the

Revolutionary War, owned one famous greyhound, named Azor. Azor was reported to be very large, and he traveled everywhere with his owner as his companion during the long, cold winter (1777 to 1778) at Valley Forge, Pennsylvania while Von Stueben and George Washington retrained the Continental Army troops.

Not until the early-to mid-1800s did America experience a large import of greyhounds from England and Ireland.

Midwest farmers primarily used greyhounds to control the jackrabbit and coyote populations to protect their crops and livestock, so the greyhounds' primary purpose during this time was hunting.

Famous Greyhound Owners

Many famous people reportedly owned greyhounds throughout history.

General George Custer is said to have owned more than 40 greyhounds. The U.S. Calvary used greyhounds as scouts to help spot Native Americans, since the greyhounds were as fast as horses. In some of Custer's writings, it is apparent he had great affection and loyalty to his hounds. Historians note that he loved to nap on the floor of his parlor with all of his greyhounds lying around him.

General Custer (sitting) with Stag and
Greyhound

On the evening of the battle at
Little Big Horn in 1876, Custer was said
to have sent his greyhounds to the
security of the city with a Calvary soldier
named James H. Kelly. Custer did not
survive this battle, but as fate would
have it, his greyhounds did.

Other renowned greyhound
owners include Cleopatra, Alexander
the Great, King Henry VIII and

Anne Boleyn, Queen Elizabeth I, and U.S. presidents John Tyler and Rutherford B. Hayes. More recently, Major League baseball player Don Mattingly, football legend Gale Sayers, singer Trent Reznor, and Charlie Watts, drummer for the Rolling Stones, all were proud greyhound owners.

A Long Pedigree Line

Many retired racing dogs have long pedigree lines. Logan's pedigree line goes back to 1780 on his mother's side.

His breeding history shows that his ancestors traveled from the UK to Ireland to Australia, back to the UK, then to the United States over the course of 220 years.

Several of Logan's male ancestors

won the Waterloo Cup in England during the nineteenth century, so his champion line is well established.

Today, adoption groups worldwide work in partnership with greyhound racetracks to assist in placing greyhounds into responsible, loving homes once they are retired.

Greyhounds as Pets

It may surprise you that greyhounds are big loungers. Although we often see them in photographs running at top speeds, when they're not running, they're lounging, which is why they are called the 45-mile per hour couch potato! They are very much at home with their families.

Greyhounds are gentle, loving, polite, eager to please, and great human companions. They are intelligent, comical and funny, and most will amuse you with their silly antics. They come in a variety of over 30 color combinations, have short coats, are clean, and shed very little. They are inside pets and do not require a lot of exercise—a walk three to four times a week is enough.

Greyhounds are not very vocal; they are laid back and do not make good watchdogs, because most everyone is their friend.

Their average life span is 12-14 years. They weigh on the average of 55 to 85 pounds and stand between 24 to 30 inches at the shoulder.

Greyhounds have graced the world for thousands of years and have been adored by many because of their endearing and docile personalities. They well deserve the respect that has been given to them throughout history.

Greyhound Adoption

Greyhound adoption groups are located in almost every state across the U.S. and also throughout Europe and Australia.

Most of these groups are non-profit and rely on donations to help rehabilitate and house the greyhounds that are retired from the racetracks, arrive from breeding kennels, or are strays.

If you would like to help a greyhound or two, consider donating funds or getting involved as a volunteer with a local greyhound adoption group.

You can make a donation online at www.greyhoundadoptiontx.org or through your local greyhound adoption group. These donations are used specifically for the greyhounds' medical care, rehabilitation, and adoption efforts.

You might also consider fostering a greyhound to discover how wonderful they are, or adopt one of these amazing resilient and loving animals.

Greyhounds will not disappoint you. They are looking for compassionate souls like you to enjoy just a little bit of love and joy while they grace this earth.

To read more about this amazing ancient dog breed and to learn more about adoption, please visit: www.greyhoundstories.com. You can also visit us on Facebook at www.facebook.com/greyhoundstories.

Additional Greyhound Stories written by Suzanne Burke will be available through www.greyhoundstories.com and directly through the Amazon.com Kindle Store, NOOK® by Barnes and Noble, and Apple iBookstore.

A portion of the profits from the purchase of this book goes directly to non-profit greyhound and galgo adoption groups worldwide. Galgos are greyhounds from Spain and are in need of homes, as are greyhounds from Australia, China, Europe, and the United States. Please contact info@greyhoundstories.com to find out how you can participate.

PROJECTS FOR CHILDREN
∂∞∽

1) Find three events or decision points in the book that could have changed the outcome of Logan's story. Share with a parent or friend what you think could have happened differently.

2) Write the beginning of Logan's story, before he starts racing. How did he grow up? How did he get trained to race? With your parents' permission, do some research on the Internet to find out more about a young racing greyhound's life.

3) Why was a home so important to Logan? Explain why it is important to everyone.

4) Describe your home and family members, including your pets. Draw a picture and write a story about the family members that are important to you.

5) Create a map of Logan's travels from Florida to Texas.

6) Write the beginning of your own life story. How does it start? What do you want to do in your lifetime?

Expand Your Vocabulary

On the next page, check out new words from the story to add to your vocabulary. Look up the meaning of each word and try using one new word a day in conversation.

Vocabulary List

Conducted	Plea
Despair	Plodding
Elite	Recounted
Eternity	Replenishing
Grueling	Retirement
Horrific	Samaritan
Instinct	Testament
Ironically	Vagabond
Jockeyed	Vast
Mesmerizing	Venture
Nightmarish	Visualize
Optimistic	Wandered
Persistent	

ABOUT THE AUTHOR

Suzanne Burke, a native of Richmond, Virginia, currently lives in a suburb of Dallas, Texas, with her retired racing greyhounds. She has more than 10 years' experience working with the greyhound breed as a volunteer for the Greyhound Adoption League of Texas. Suzanne also has more than 15 years' experience in the information technology field in project management and technical writing.

Photographers/Graphic Design

Shawn Fernandez

Shawn Fernandez is an award-winning producer and editor in the film and television industry. He also works in motion graphics design and photography. He lives in Dallas, Texas.

John Hudson

John Hudson of John Hudson Photography has provided award-winning photojournalistic, traditional, and candid photography throughout Texas and the United States since 1989. He lives in Dallas, Texas.

Editors

Leslie Thompson and Lee Weaver

Special Thanks

Thank you to the following people who provided technical support on this project:

Bob Brooks, Eric Burke, Jeff Burke, Steve Burke, Tim Burke, Barbara Christian, Sammye Conway, Colleen Corbett, Cheryl Daniel, Ingrid Dinsmore, Lisa Gits, Douglas Haynes, Lia Haynes, John McQuade, Susie McQuade, Edward Pittman, Sara Ramadan, Sarah Somers, Rita Wulke.

14757193R00066

Made in the USA
Charleston, SC
29 September 2012